1

A Whisper of the Romantic in the Eye of God

A Spiritual Awakening in Poetry

ISBN 978-0-9559848-0-8

Author:

Lisa Marie Gabriel

Published in the UK

First Edition September 2008

The cover design of this book uses an X Ray image of the Eye of God Nebula, this was produced by the Spitzer telescope. It is one of many incredibly beautiful space photos from NASA which are thankfully in the public domain.

4

2005 – 2008

A time of richness, it was....

A time of fertile imaginings....

A time of new dreams and old understanding....

A time of new acceptance and old rejection, for shedding both fear and deception....

A time of awakening from and into complete innocence....

A new awakening to Love and Pain....

How do you represent a journey in poetry? How do you speak of spiritual awakening? Do you present every twist and turn of the creative and emotional path, or only those you would share without a blush? The truth lies somewhere between the two, otherwise nothing would ever be printed, and in this collection I have striven to be creatively honest without an excess of Sturm and Drang. Maybe in future years I will produce "a complete works" (if it can ever be complete) or maybe release more slim volumes and leave the editing to others. For now, those who want more are recommended to my first two books.

In Remembrance of Future Present,

ISBN 1 905126 24 7

Love From The Ashes – Seasons in the Fire

ISBN 1 905126 54 9

Published by Poetry Monthly Press.

(poetrymonthly@btinternet.com)

This book is dedicated with Love to all my friends and family and to all those worldwide for whom Love is the sole (soul) answer. We are but a whisper of the romantic in the Eye of God! Most especially it is dedicated to Jewels who exemplifies Love in every action....

Outside

Outside,

A gentle rain is falling.

The chorus of birdsong

Tells of yet another day

Dawning,

But no dream of Love fulfilled in you.

Inside,

The gentle rain within my heart

Reminds me how I feel for you

And how I need to Be

With you -

A part of every joy and pain

And passing moment....

With you,

I felt my spirit leap

And sing the songs of Hope

And reach for Paradise

Knowing that part of me,

Part of God within us both.

Silence

Is not an option that I cherish -

Not to know or share

That Wholeness of the Spirit

Found in Love,

Your eyes

The very window of my Soul....

Love me with gentleness

Love me with gentleness, not with the storm

Of passion that consumes all in its way.

For I am like the seed that flies on the wind,

My soul seeks finer soil in which to grow

And you might grasp too hard

And crush the flower before it's time in May.

Love me with contentment, not with fear of loss

For what we have is not and never can be lost

Though winds of change will take me on

To where I have to fly alone....

Know in my heart there'll always be a special place

For you, and love that never counted cost....

Love me with compassion, for all the time

I gave to you, and never counted wholly mine.

The hours spent together in that common dream

And how I helped your spirits lift when others left them low.

For how I gave my heart and mind to help you win

So that once more, for you, the sun could shine.

Love me with detachment, not with chains,

For now a path I have to find in me

That takes me into lands uncharted now -

Where freedom is the key to my new life.

Commitment to another is the path I seek - so, let me go,

And know, to love me, you must set me free.

Catching the dream from far beyond….

Catching the dream from far beyond….

That passes through, mere whisper to the soul, from something great.

That still, small voice that is so often drowned

By Life's necessities, its rush and manic state.

Catching the hope of far beyond....

The dream we all should dare, if time there be,

The legacy we're offered, one and all,

If only we should dare to dream and set it free.

Catching the moment sent from far beyond...

Before its lost forever in the haze of thought

That occupies each second of our human span,

That stifles our awareness and brings dreams to nought.

Catching the spirit lent from far beyond....

Before it flies unnoticed to another realm;

Lighting the present with a fleeting glimpse of Love -

That's poetry, with body, mind and spirit at the helm....

Finding the Road to Freedom.

Sometimes we struggle far too hard,

The mind we send from place to place,

And choice becomes impossible,

Once veiled behind confusion's face.

To know ones self takes inner peace

And then detachment grants release.

And when we care, as care we must,

Our inner voice will often fail

And memories of past misdeeds

Can make us seem beyond the pale.

The answer could be "Just let go"

But who am I to tell you so?

Perhaps it seems that giving in

And tracking back is hard to do.

That vulnerable to guilt we shake

Upon the threshold of the new.

Perhaps we need to face those fears,

Work through the grief and shed some tears?

Perhaps in order to be free,

We once again must face those ties,

The pains and hardship that we fled;

The mind can tell such subtle lies....

So, to be free, must we again

Return and risk that loving chain?

And only in that giving self,

That love of such a hurting kind

Can we discover who we are

For pure avoidance makes us blind....

So, face the challenge of the past?

By this, be truly free at last....

Time - present - tide flows....

Fly to me in the darkness like a moth to a velvet flame.

The beat of your gentle wings will touch my heart.

Say that you're with me always, that you own no shame,

That time and tide alone are all that keep our souls apart.

Speak to me in the shadows as you spoke to me once before,

Speak to my heart as one who treasures simple things.

Why should you fear me? Could I ever love you more?

Love, could I give you less than what I own my spirit sings?

Touch me in silent moments when the world is fast asleep,

When, sitting alone, I wonder at Love's hidden schemes.

Had I but said "I love you", what whirlwinds could I reap?

Simply, I trust that time and tide are merely dreams....

In the Wolds, by Tealby

Today my heart and I sped through the Wolds,

You smiled for me, your gentle voice in mind,

I spoke to you of love, both heart and soul,

And in that Love both Heart and Soul were joined....

Our stars shine with a rainbow to protect you,

Our sun will not forget to play his part,

And I will never leave you, or reject you,

How could I hurt the one that owns my heart?

The birds were singing, so I stopped to listen

And savour music from the trees above,

Who bent to share the secret, leaves all glistened

With a special radiance, meant just for you my love....

Your smile was in the sun, I felt it fill me,

And feed the birds their song and then I knew

Whatever Time may bring, Love will not kill me,

This love is unconditional and true....

A Wish for all my Friends....

Gently, my heart flies out to you -

In flight with the songs of a thousand years

And when your dreams meet the morning glow

May love and peace dissolve your fears.

May you dance in the stream of a thousand lives

And live as you never lived before;

Embrace each other in new-found joy

And never want for hope, and more....

May your songs be the songs of freedom

And compassion fill your days....

May you never stumble unhappy paths

Nor beauty cease to amaze.

May you know the joy that belongs to all

To God, to Man, to Creation whole -

For we are One, and we have won,

Embracing Love within the Soul....

To GM

The journey through our life is all we need to own.

The end is undetermined, but our goal's in sight.

We are on track each moment, sharing as we go,

Each obstacle we conquer brings us closer to the light.

Believing now that we are one will see us through

And taking ownership of all the trials we passed;

As every moment we stood up for what is true

We'll both be winners when we reach the end at last.

We carry hopes and dreams of friends along the way

A common need for justice and for peace - that shining light -

Whoever wins the race, we have the right to say

Our journey taught us much - we saw no need to fight.

Remember this, my friend, and to yourself be true,

Both winners in the end, I share so many dreams with you !

A Child at the Sea....

(For Gilly on her birthday at Garwick....)

Somewhere a clock chimes three....

A seagull's cry,

Like plaintive ghost,

Pierces a slow dawning sky,

And here I lie.....

A child suspended,

Caught in that magic hour 'twixt night and day.

Nor wake, nor sleep,

But race the innocent dreams of freedom.....

And in my mind,

So old in one so young,

Down to the pebble beach I fly....

The scent of the breeze,

Seductive,

Fragrance of shellfish, tar, and the salt sea,

Plays havoc with my senses.

The boats lie idle,

Captains roll the deep sleep of sated pleasure,

Dreaming of rum, and ale,

And Siren songs of the night before....

A symphony of shingle;

Waves pulling,

And the rush and roar

Of tide on stone,

Soft water - tunnelling ancient rock -

Moulds, shapes and plays;

Itself a child on some forgotten shore.....

As lone crabs stalk,

Anemones flower.....

What child of time

Could ever wish for more?

Nurtured through the primetime....

My parents nurtured me

Through the primetime of youth;

Gave me their all...

Denying only independence -

Lovingly, they tried to steer me

Where I could not go in truth...

With love, my first family

Bequeathed to me their hopes and fears

Which then became my own reality.

A fragile spirit, just a pale reflection;

Afraid of who I might become,

The ties of love which bound me

And the darker beauty of my imperfection,

I hid myself away.

Banished from the world,

My heart denied fruition -

A plant denied the warmth of Day....

My second family, no longer strangers,

Led me through my darkest hours -

Grief coursing, flooding every artery

In sullen haemorrhage

For such great loss of time and love...

They healed me through each crisis;

Fanned the flame but held me fast,

Secure, through every new and wild catharsis.

Through the rebirth of my inner truth

They loved me and in that support,

Protecting from the past,

Accepting fully, gladly, who I am,

They gifted me with Youth.

Caressing through imagined dangers

This, my new identity.

In Unconditional Love,

With open heart and mind's full trust,

They nurtured me.

By the River.....

And you should know

How deep this heart

With loving

Fills each perfect day....

Azure skies,

Cloud-flecked white,

Bird song blessed,

And the river

Winding purposefully,

Searchingly....

Trees,

Green vestured,

Spear both moon-drenched,

Coal deep Heavens

And day bright robe of Madonna.

Ancient and sprawling,

A willow speaks peacefully,

Alone,

Huge,

Benign, wise and gentle,

His bark shaggy,

Centuries worn of stillness,

Wind and water.

Incandescent flowers,

Pin prick lights,

Camera Obscura

Of saffron, rose and lilac,

Bright-hued thrones of wildness

Where bees hum heavy

In impossible flight.

Hovering butterflies probe

The hearts of sweetness,

Welcomed by each loving host....

By the river

You walk the towpath of this flowing mind,

Welcomed also,

Take my hand -

I ask no more

Than you would wish to give....

Safe, secure,

At peace with life and laughter.

So should you know

How deep this heart

With love and laughter

Greets each perfect day....

I moved from Love - to love -

I moved from Love - to love -

Just like a moth to flame,

Seeking I knew not what -

Direction lacking,

Unfulfilled, my spirit drained -

Somehow all lovers were the same...

Then I was drawn to you,

But learned that I must give you space,

And doubt became a fire;

Consuming passion

Seared a heart both new and free,

I did not understand my place...

I moved from doubt to hope,

Learning to love my inner truth.

Although I feared you lost to me,

Alone I stumbled

On a narrow path that led me

Back to innocence and youth...

And in that innocence

I learned that Love is always right,

Will never count the cost,

But freely speak its Name aloud -

Asks nothing more, nor less,

But gently moves from Love to Light...

A Ship Therein...

My heart belongs to sea and sky,

Where tall ships

Plough their silken furrows

Through soft fields of indigo and blue

And seagulls cry,

Proclaiming resting place

On languid cliff tops

Drifting by...

My heart belongs to sea and breeze,

Where playful waves

Whip froth of velvet white

Through agitated silken green

And smiling

I am caught by foam caress,

It's gentle promise

Soothing me...

My heart belongs to sea and tides,

Where moonbeams

Capture painted jewels

On bible black unfathomed deep,

Elusive gems;

A glint in Heaven's eye

That, teasing, steals my soul besides…

And sailing here beneath these stars,

At one with moon and mystery,

With heart so light my spirit sings -

I would not - could not - sleep

And waste a moment of this sacred night

Wherein my heart belongs, and soul takes flight,

A loving gift to sea and tides….

Twin Flames….

Flaming twins we started and flaming twins we stayed.

Each to the other mirrored all the warts that Karma made.

As frightened by my aspects you changed your hour of birth,

I saw in stark intensity my Heavenly Twin on Earth.

It never should have come to this, a mess of yin and yang,

Loved by a part-time poet who stuttered Sturm und Drang

And just as sweet Narcissus did, I saw myself and fell -

Mistaken I saw Heaven but my twin saw only Hell!

Like fireflies we hovered, each flirting in the light,

Until the glass was shattered to reveal a gem more bright.

I hope you never wonder when the nights grow cold and wild

What might have been if flaming twin had not seemed flaming child,

Had Innocence not shocked you as your Lamb failed to impress,

Then Honesty not mocked you making Lion heart seem less!

Jealousy.

The white cat stamped…

The grey cat closed his eyes

And purred.

He'd spoken much of Love,

Though no word passed his lips;

Aloud, for all to hear,

He crooned and chirped

And now Love's Serenade had won reward…

The white cat stamped…

In blue-eyed innocence,

Diana Dors,

Intense and sultry in her silver fur,

Outrage arrayed in velvet,

She pawed the ground… .

The white cat stamped…

She raised her pretty voice,

Indignation

Plain for all to see;

And written there

In show of fur -

"You'll have no other god but me…"

Flow With Me Always….

Flow with me always,

Swift running streams -

Laughing, sing your joy

Past boulders;

Sparkling, clean and pure,

So gently wear

Each stone

Loving as you flow

And as I love…

Speak with me always,

Song birds in the night -

Soft your gift at twilight -

Soothing music

Nourish heart and soul

With hope;

Break down these silent walls

And sing my Love…

Stay with me always,

Gentle breezes;

Caressing light and shade

Through leaves that bend and kneel

To One

Who knows my heart -

I know

Love calls you to this

Heart you own…

Soft Words, In Calm Moments....

You come to me

In quiet moments

Between sleep and wakefulness,

When the world outside

Is dark with the Promise

Of New Day.

When I am most alone,

Then you are there at night

To guide....

My Muse,

Child of the Light,

My Hope,

My Love

And dearest Friend....

So stay

And, if my words

Can ever touch you,

Knowing , as I do,

Life's challenges

Weigh heavy on your gentle soul,

Then Sweet the touch,

And hope that Love

Which makes us whole

May find you -

Bringing Joy and Peace to one

Who gives so much…

The Dreamtime….

Dozing,

In the full Expectancy

Of nothing more

Than what I own is mine to give,

What Worlds do I create?

Half sleeping,

Half awake,

In perfect pleasure

As I travel on?

Do not wake me,

Do not cut me off from Life,

For Joy is here -

And in this hour is Peace.

This is the Dreamtime,

I, the Dreamer,

Let me sleep

Creating Worlds of Love...

Without the Rain....

Without -

The Rain,

Which loving drives

The sap of Life

And living;

Growth and rebirth find

Regenerating Light,

Suffusing green which heals us

In our giving....

Without -

The Rain,

These knowing trees

Reflect our Love

And Laughter;

Age and Wisdom caught

In root and ancient bark

Recording tales for all to hear

Long after....

Without -

The Rain

Calls living Hope

From old desires,

Leaves sharing

Life in tender green

Spring promises of love,

Desiring inner Peace - content

In caring....

In May....

In May I suffer England's temper gladly,

Her changing mood

As violent rain

Is stilled in sunshine's glory....

Now in the silence,

Mitigated only by

The softest touch of showers,

Birds sing;

Noisy,

A rich choir,

Treble voices crowning Woodland

With bold Love and Laughter.

Distant hills,

Soft satin sheets

Of saffron and of ochre

Expose Her

Through a veil of verdant trees -

All these I suffer!

White floral umbrellas

Lend their shelter

To distracted bees

Bereft, for now, of nectar

As, iridescent ,

In the hedgerow,

Blossom mocks....

A loping fox takes stock

Pauses an instant,

Then, intense and fearless,

Takes his leave

For wilder passions…

All these I suffer gladly!

A distant village

Cradled in the hillside's

Soothing arms;

Solemn silhouette -

A row of pines -

Caresses

Innocent cloud strewn skies.

All these things, tender,

Hold me in embrace

Of England's fickle Glory

In the Spring

And lead me on to dream

A landscape softer yet -

Embraced by you…

Sea of Memory....

Waves tremble,

Pulsing

On the dark granite Ocean

That is my mind.

A fond tide stirs them,

This, my love for you,

Will never end…

Hold me

Just an instant in your thoughts,

That I might feel once more

The tender hand of memory

On this -

Faint Heart of Darkness …

Think of me awhile with love,

So that your voice

May fill my soul with light -

And laughter -

As I strive to catch the Dream

That I would share

With One -

A vital part of me -

Who drives the steady

Force of Love

Through time, space

And Eternity

Until it finds its Peace

With You....

The Minstrel and the Bard

Noon....

And a piper at the Gates of Love,

Assured and unselfconscious,

Tells of a bittern

Who died by the lake -

Frozen -

Beak unable

To penetrate the ice....

Sweet, the Uillean pipes

Croon dark lament

By stone on stone....

I am taken up

On these bold Celtic wings.

Do not resist!

My heart was always yours

For the taking.

My soul wants to fly -

To penetrate the ice

Of Lincoln's noonday sun

And drink the sweet waters

Of Freedom....

I long to fly to you,

My distant love,

And sing my dreams....

Long to share

This Flight

With you....

And now

The music changes to a reel -

My feet

Invited to the Dance!

These pipes, this piper,

Weave their magic well....

By this Cathedral

Ancient, strong in ritual and romance,

We share a pagan mirth!

The Minstrel and the Bard

Who meet by chance -

I miss you now,

But will not die of Love -

Nor try to dance!

In Remembrance Of Future Present...

On the sacred touch

Of a Summer breeze,

Fresh

To a heart in Winter slumber,

Flows such warm fragrance...

Sweet Life renewed

In tender caress -

And in this Wave of Love

I gladly swim

I sing

Through the Heart of darkness;

Dance

In the Stream

Of a thousand lives -

Breathe

The deep mystery of Renewal.

Faith is my rock

And Love?

Passion no longer

My hiding place -

But joy - this fountain of Light

And Summer laughter…

And shall I taste the Promise

Of things to come?

Here, in this space of simply being?

Tranquillity…

The touch of an Angel's wing

Unknown to me -

Unknowing -

Folds my soul

In such a fond embrace

And in soft kiss

Reveals

Just Who I am…

Love Is....

Love is -

Simply as it is -

No more, nor less....

A touch -

Words whispered low

I must confess;

And yet in darkest night

It shines - a lasting glow.

Perhaps it leads to greater Love?

Perhaps you know...

Love is -

Simply as it is -

A joy received

This gift that two can share

I once believed;

And yet

In light of day

It grows - still radiant there.

A dream that leads us all to Light?

If we but care...

Love is -

Simply as it is -

Eternal Youth...

A hope of sweet release

The only Truth;

So still

This restless heart

And let all troubles cease.

In Love, we make our world anew -

The Road to Peace...

Nothing More Than This....

Let me take your hand...

On this journey

We will tread a tender path

Deep down

Into the Heart

And find quiet space.

A forest way -

Fresh smell of pine -

Not a soul in sight,

Just you and I....

Deep down

Into my heart

Where rivers run -

Silent and clear -

Fast-flowing past boulders;

Sandy banks -

Beaches in miniature -

Invite us to bathe

In silence....

Deep down

Where mountains touch sky

Speak ageless wisdom,

Love and patience -

Snow-capped -

Fresh in majesty....

Deep down

To this shady grove

Where, sweet smelling,

Wild flowers raise tiny heads

In praise of Light....

Music around us,

Soothing and peaceful,

No more than the rustling

Of branches in the wind....

Birds sing

And Sun shines

Dappled through leaves

On soft grass

Where we lie....

Deep down

To this sacred place....

 Here I shed

The frustrations of traffic,

The riot of sound and sensation

As a snake sheds its skin

In the soothing green....

Take my hand -

With you,

Happy to Be,

I will dance

Through Dreamtime

And we will be free....

On Wings of Fire

Lift me !

Take me to the Heights

That only Love can know...

Together we will fly

So swiftly

On the Wings of Love itself.

I will not weigh you down

My joy will fuel this flight

And in our wild adventure

We will find the Light.

Touch me

To my deepest Heart

Where only Truth can live.

Speak to me in Kindness

So gently -

Find my spirit whole and new.

I will not ask "Forever!"

Nor seek to change a thing.

Pure Love, the Music of the Soul,

Will make our Spirit sing.

Hold me

In the arms of Love

And I will know true Peace

Which Joy alone can bring.

So often

In my Dream I felt you there

If Dreams were real

And you would share this Night,

Enchanted, I would see you smile

And feel your Radiance lead me into Light!

I Am Renewed By Love

I am renewed by Love.

I am renewed

By the smile on your face,

By the breeze which cools

In a soft embrace,

By the touch of the Sun

As it takes me

Home to rest awhile….

I am renewed by Love.

I am reclaimed in Love.

I am reclaimed

By the Peace in my Heart,

By the Light in your eyes

Which fills my Day

As new Dreams arise,

And they bring me

Hope of sweet release....

I am reclaimed by Love.

I am reborn in Love,

I am reborn

From the Night with the One,

Such a part of my Soul....

We have waited so long,

Now united and Whole

In the spirit of Peace -

So healing, so bright -

I am reborn in Light!

My Muse....

Softly treading in the night,

He croons his love in velvet tone.

His eyes, so deep and knowing,

Understand my very soul....

My Muse has grown

So handsome in my sight!

My Emperor, yet humble,

Follows every move I make;

My every whim he bends to -

Every path he has to take!

Once, long ago, his beauty

Went unrecognised, unknown,

His needs, so pure and simple

Were unnoticed, never met.

Once loved, now left alone

And kept but out of Duty,

He languished on a trash can

Shabby coated in the rain

'Til rescued by an Angel

Who released him from his pain....

Now Time and patient love

Have brought glory to his face.

As confidence increased

He grew to love and trust.

My Muse has found his place,

My gift from Heaven above

What greater Mews is Max

Who serenades me in the night -

For such reward is Love

When felt so deeply at first sight!

Lines Written After Kahlil Gibran

Love, your Voice is Music

My ears had ceased to hear;

To sounds so sweet

I sing once more

And I no longer fear.

You are like the Mountain Heights

That marry Earth and Sky -

To reach you

I must climb again

Catch clouds as they drift by....

For only from the Darkness

Could I aspire to Light;

Such brightness,

Lifting Heart and Soul

From suffocating Night.

Once chained to Earth by links of Fire,

My Spirit seeks romance -

Love binds no more,

My limbs are light -

Invite my Heart to dance!

In Truth, not knowing who I am,

I gave all Hope away

And now reclaimed

I seek your Light

To brighten glorious Day.

Calm through my Death of Being,

Such Baptism of Fire,

Reborn in Love

I dare to Dream –

To seek my Heart's desire....

I travel within

I travel within - I need no more

Than the emblems of my trade.

My music and my poetry are all I take

I leave behind my past

With all mistakes that I have made.

Who knows where Love will lead me

In a world of grief and sin?

You travel the world, dear friend,

I travel within.

I travel within and darkness waits

To embrace a soul in pain

But Hope protects and Faith sustains me

Through to journey's end.

No fear, though chilled by wind and rain -

No Sun as yet, but Light will dawn

Alone, but steady, I begin -

Love will not leave me standing here -

I travel within.

I travel within and feel the pace

Pick me up and lift me higher

And any obstacles melt away -

Illusions - I am free at last

From pain of unfulfilled desire.

I wonder if our paths will cross?

If so, take Friendship's hand -

You travel the world to seek, my friend,

I seek to understand...

In A Quiet Time

I will not write darkly

In this quiet space where time and tide

Seem at standstill....

For me, the Present is a race

To fill the Parting Glass

Before I taste Eternity -

But in this cold time

I live to dream -

Think kindly of me.

I will not write darkly

Of empty, silent days without Truth

For Darkness chains me down....

I would be free!

Pure Love seeks only Light!

I ask no more than this -

The future will be bright

And we will know

No more of pain.

On Such A Night

To lie together 'neath the stars

On such a night as this....

I touch your hand - you hold my heart -

My gift of Love and Trust.

Behind us, loss, before us, life;

We share both pain and bliss

On such a night,

Among the stars,

Content with Starlight's kiss....

I'm lost! Imagine how immense

Our Universe, grown small

Beside you here - your hand in mine -

As One, when One is All….

So great a Knowledge stills my heart;

I scarce can breathe for Awe….

On such a night,

Beneath the stars,

Renewed at Heaven's Door….

And now is not the time

And now is not the time for love

It is time to listen

To breezes that rustle green branches

As birds sing in the trees

And the Sun plays shadow theatre

Through the hungry leaves.

Now is not the time for love,

Yet this is love….

Now is not the time to plan

For who can say where life will lead?

The present time,

A quiet space in which we grow

Through grace to understand -

From pain to conscious love.

Reflecting all

And lifting in Love's power.

Where hope and joy seem distant

They are never far away....

And now is not a time of loss....

This time

Fills me with wonder.

These gifts you gave -

These words that run so swift -

A crystal spring that feeds

A clear renewing stream....

These waters run

Through the dark forested mind.

These waters run

Through the shadows,

Deep and treacherous,

Tracing my rebirth.

I follow a winding path,

Narrow,

That leads me from confusion

To this, my Inner Self,

Who loves so much

But knows so well

I share my path with no one

But will never be alone....

Dance For Dreama

For You

I will always dance, my love,

Through the trials of life

And the fire of pain,

And the Joy of the Dance

Will see us through

As we dance together

Through Sun and Rain...

For You

I will always dance, my love,

When the skies are dark

And the nights are long,

And the Joy of the Dance

Will lift us high

As we learn to sing

A different song...

For You

I will always dance, my love,

Through this Heart of Love

To the Rainbow's End,

And the Joy of Love

I will sing for you

As I dance through Life

With Hope, Sweet Friend....

Loneliest of Trees

The willow bends

Beneath the weight of years.

Tears of late, and age long

Spent in silent solitude,

She never poured on sunbeams' wings…

"Shame" cry swallows for past pains,

"Only a fool will strive for perfect peace -

Shame to call no compromise -

We swallows fly for Spring!"

In Winter dreams the tree's dark heart

In lighter wood

Lies hidden, long since won,

She heeds not what her soul cries out

But acts as calmly bidden

By her Life and Lord, the Sun….

"Of all the trees

That Love might plant and tend

The willow wears the lightest shade -

And yet my branches,

Sagging, weep and bend

In some too distant hilly glade.

All plants must strive

Towards their Sun - as I -

Yet God, our keeper, knew

The strongest heart will bend to Fate -

In darkness then I grew"....

Of all the trees that Love might plant

The willow most must bend

But once the tree grew strong and straight

Will yet again!

The wind through smiling leaves

Will sing of Life's true love, in joy,

If Sun can prove he loves her....

The willow, dark and silent,

Bends with time,

Though Hope has never left,

Can never leave, the straining leaves;

The bowing, lacy wands that hang,

The grace that nature gave to elder Youth;

The longing for the unattainable -

The only Eden -

That of all her longing speaks most Truth.

The willow bends with love

And love has never left the smiling leaves -

Or once the heart

Which strives to see the Sun,

To feel his warmth, his life, his love -

With him at last to be at one -

She weeps for distance soon to cease...

Ah! Loneliest of trees!

This River, And Soft Wings' Embrace....

Until your dreams

Call to reality

Then soft,

Will I come in the Night

And Spirit Wings of Love

Will touch your sleeping face,

Caress and brush away your tears;

Sow soft, pink flowers

On pallid fields, Twin Roses,

Fragrant of the Heart's Desire

And Inner Peace....

 Till then,

This River of Hope,

Chaste, protecting,

Winds between us

Washing clean

All sorrows past.

It purifies my heart,

Declares a Love

That knows no boundaries,

Can tell no lies

And asks no more

Than Peace -

Until that day,

Your Dreams

May touch my own....

To hold you in my arms

And like young Eagles

Learn to soar,

Safe folded,

In these Wings' Embrace...

Rose After Rain....

So delicate,

The touch and feel of softened velvet;

Crimson, light of air....

Caressing raindrops,

Joy's reflection there,

A gentle prism shatters Day

And rainbows dance for us to share....

So say farewell to grief and pain

And bend to kiss Rose after Rain....

So beautiful,

The Soul's own gift of Love and Trust

Will lift me to the Light....

Love has me reeling

Heart overwhelmed by such a sight....

A loving Spirit lending Hope

And Strength, I leave the long, dark Night....

Nothing to lose - Heaven to gain -

I dream of Love, Rose after Rain....

For Love Is not A Place.....

For Love

Is not a place

Where I would go....

Nor time the lonely hours,

Nor pace the room

In hopes the phone might ring....

Nor weep within my heart

And wish it were not so....

One call, and then

My heart would sing?

No, Love is not a place

Where I would go....

I said

I would not lose control;

I could not love again.

Rash words,

From inner fear

This heart grown vulnerable,

Reluctant now to trust...

And yet within the Soul

Can be no pain....

Lack of control?

Do flowers control the Sun?

Is wind at grasses' whim?

Do seas spin tides

Upon the moon?

I do not know....

Know only this is so

Love is a place

Where wise men will not go....

But say

That this is nothing?

That I cannot do.

As I lie here

I drink the Sun

Though distant now

I share with you....

Taste of Life around me,

Sense a future bright

With promise of the New....

Take from this heart

Whatever strength you need

I ask not that you give

Or that you feel

What is not yours to own,

But simply,

Live

If Love is not a place

Where you would go....

 No foolish dreams,

No bold desire,

No wish for full control.

Free of ties that bind -

Free of controlling mind -

Free now to follow this,

My heart and soul;

I say to all

Who've loved and lost,

Go with the flow....

As Love is slow to chide,

Swift to forgive -

A place

Where I would gladly go....

 For in this place of stillness,

Calm and free,

Knowing peace and hope

That Love

Somehow

Has given me;

Here lies

The only true reality....

And in this stillness,

Conflict past,

The pain of yesterday

Grown pale

And somehow very small.

I let go fear,

And seeds of hope I sow

For good or ill,

For all that counts is now -

This present -

Bright and vast -

Love is the only place

That I would gladly go....

My Laugharne Love....

"Ydych chi'n eisiau yn arall, Cariad?"

"We do not 'ave such truck with Nationalists here,

The English do not like it!"

Laughing, we English, here in Brown's Hotel,

Wallpaper stained and faded - long unchanged -

Giggle through our warm, Welsh bitter beer.

Toast the Man, resplendent in old photograph,

As, playing cards, he too laughs with old regulars.

Then, like hungry sparrows, flock We to the Shed.

Young Lion crouches, mane a sail aflame,

Romp, smiling Beauty at his side

He rolls a slimline Jazz - caring Llareggub!

Then to the glass pained door

With smoke paned eyes squeezed tight on Faith....

Dark laden, dusty as Caitlin left it thus,

On desk, a bottle now undrained,

Typewriter silent as the grave,

Pencils bask with cigarettes now cold

And paper balls on desk and floor;

Left alone one final time

Just as the day it was He died

And Music left the Bay....

Over Sir John's Hill clouds are scudding;

We small birds of the Bay seek shelter from their tears....

Dilly, dilly! Come we to die beneath this Hawk's shadow?

We four, sequestered within wooden pillars,

Come to live!

The Jazz is mine, I offer it to Sea and Sky,

Reach in my jacket, twist the metal cap,

Savour the music of the moment....

"Ydych chi'n eisiau yn arall, Cariad?"

I whisper to the silent tide beneath.

The Hawk on Fire hangs still,

The Famous Grouse takes flight,

An offering to you,

My Laugharne Love....

A Broken Piano.

A colour missing....

Dark abyss

In these infinite shades of blue....

This note -

Centred in the keyboard -

Softest touch falling into Nothing

But longing,

Touches the void!

Can I sing that missing note?

Yes!

Hear my voice

Through shades of Being?

Touching, it stands alone,

Harmony marred only by loss...

This Voice is not mechanical -

Was never automatic in the scheme of things....

This Life,

My words;

A meditation on Love;

How this alone remains

When missing notes,

Denied,

Unheard,

Are amplified by Silence....

Three Sea Pictures

Waves shimmer, dancing, playful, into shore -

Toss driftwood, flotsam, on the sands;

Found objects catch my eye,

Touch Heart and Soul

With shadow promise, sweet,

Of unknown places - offer fleeting

Glimpses of a world I wish to try;

Bystander still, yet reaching out my hand

Until they leave me high and dry....

And then, a steady tide that ebbs and flows

Surrounds, predictable,

Safe harbour, calling home

To sanctuary - free from harm -

No pain - soft waters these -

Lap gentle round my bows....

Such calm before each storm and after,

When my courage fails, helps float again

All dreams of love and laughter....

Skies darken, choke back rain like tears

As I float free on fickle tide....

Waves tower as this battered hull

Is rocked in turn by hope and fear.

So, Brave Hearts hardly dare

To venture on such storm tossed seas,

To ride the mountainous swell ?

I must! Your message calls my Soul

To sail all storms in Trust....

Old Slippers....

Ornaments upon a shelf;

Together,

Not opposing ends,

They sit....

She -

Tall and thin

And somewhat prim -

Elegant,

An elderly Cleopatra

Rules the Nile.

He -

Short and round,

Relaxed and slumped

Into his chair,

A faithful, silent hound

Who guards his Queen.

An hour passes,

Maybe two -

And not a precious word is spent;

Both poised,

And steel-rimmed spectacles

Lend power

To fading sight.

They clutch twin puzzle books,

Pens poised,

Scratch at the surface tension

Punctuated only

As they pause

To finger cold French fries.

Yet we devour our meal

As we devour life -

Colin cracks a joke,

I laugh,

We share our dreams....

I nudge his knee

At first he does not see.

Then....

"What would they do

If one should die?"

He asks....

She finishes her puzzle first.

"There, that one was easy!

How are you?"

Conversation easily put on,

Like old slippers....

Nothing troubling there -

And so, for such,

Is Love....

Apricot

You tumble chaotic into my dreams

With the rustle of paper,

Scratching away in dark corners

Where spiders fall prey

To your happy search.

Himalayan goddess!

You charm such joy

From these high passes

Where no man could tread.

Then,

THUD!

The day is shattered

By the thunder footfall

Of such delicate feet

And the click of cellulose.

Like Pele, you dive

And dribble your ball,

This mouse,

Your prey.

Bleary-eyed,

So early in the day

I roll sweet in avoidance....

Sandpaper softly scours my cheek,

Your tongue....

Roughly,

You kiss my eyes to wake,

You chew my hair....

How can I grudge a second

Of this Summer Sunday morning?

Laughing, I rise....

I lift you in my arms

And hug my Woolly Bear!

In Love....

In Love,

I seek full trust,

Through honesty,

Acceptance of my truth

And yours....

Nothing withheld,

No secrets -

Just the words

That make us whole,

That open doors....

For then

I'd give my heart,

So freely won

So long ago by you

And gain

The joy I seek -

No sorrow -

Just the gift

That frees each soul

From grief and pain....

Night Reflections....

A quiet house....

Distant music

And the ticking of a clock –

Resonant –

A cat purrs and the rumble of an engine

Echoes love....

The rain has stopped now;

Tears falling from the sky....

But were they tears of grief or joy?

Who knows....

Yet all is well....

And do we know

Within these quiet walls

Of love and pain?

How show

The joy of giving

Without fear of loss?

This freedom is a gift!

Tonight,

Words fail me....

I am drawn to act!

To give – to love....

Each sound a symphony....

Such silent nights as these

Once drew down fear.

No fear now in this moment,

Just awareness of this truth –

I am that I am....

No more, no less....

There's nothing can be taken

That I would not freely give.

There's nothing I would take

That changes anything

Within this quiet space

Where all I own

Is peace....

Sunrise....

When you come to me

In those silent moments of my choosing,

Ring my body with your light.

Open,

Tingling with awareness

Of all that was -

And is -

And shall be,

Then shall I know

That star within me

Burn so bright –

So fierce that I can scarce hold on

Yet face down fear

And turn its strength to healing....

What is given

Never shall be lost

Love will not find me wanting

In this stillness...

The White Room....

Meanwhile,

In the I-ness of this eternal minute,

I watch paint dry,

White on white;

Disappearing into vast one-ness

Of which I have no concept....

Was it the moment we stood;

Two souls seemed to me as one

Across a white room?

I felt the touch

Of another heart on mine,

Longed for soft warmness

On that winter night....

When did I lose the plot?

When I melted in your smile,

Or when, unbidden,

Gave too much of Love and Light?

In that brief moment,

Lost,

Should I have told you more?

Risked all I had?

So little -

Yet it seemed so much -

Gambled it all

On the sharing

Of unspoken dreams -

A nervous touch?

Meanwhile,

In the eternal I-ness of this minute

I watch the paint dry,

White on white -

Disappearing

Into the vast white One-ness

Of a dream

You could not understand....

Feral Love....

Greedy for leftover love,

He steals into our passageway;

Black, burr bedraggled,

Seeking Persian leavings....

One ear almost two,

Socks and vest immaculate -

New fallen snow....

Nobility in shabbiness!

Taking guard upon the roof,

Sentry to Need,

He pauses, watchful;

Every in and out an opportunity.

Joyful,

He bumps his massive head -

Each venture and return he greets....

Pampered once perhaps,

Now sadly lost,

He craves the love he senses....

Our neighbour's in the yard!

"He will not let me pass!"

The little panther has her cornered....

Later she tells her friend -

"Our neighbour feeds him"

He scratched her once,

When in desperate bid for warmth

He raked her tights as cats will do....

"He's such a nuisance!"

Nuisance,

Screwball, as we call him,

Shuts his eyes....

He purrs,

Dreaming of tasty offerings left

When Fear subsides

And her Compassion stirs....

Alligator....

Leaving this safe haven,

My pool,

Where I lay silent for so long

I calmly glide....

Seeking no conflict,

I swim tranquil,

Driven by an inner voice

That soothes my fear.

Taking only what I need

With no desire to lay up stores

Against some mythic drought,

Peaceful, I watch my prey

And sated let it pass

Upon its own foray

In this liquid Universe.

I guarded my young -

Fiercely, as a mother should -

Now they must find their way….

My mission now,

Delighting purely in the freedom

Of the running stream,

Is simply….

Be….

Drawing the warmth

From unknown worlds above;

The sun upon my back,

This balm of cooler waters

Adding lustre to my skin.

Scales sparkle!

Rainbows in the light's reflected love!

Into the darker eddies

Flowing, safe,

At peace with inner purpose,

No more need to hide....

Amberley.

What if your lion's mane,

Your fierce owl eyes

And griffin posture

Offer feline threat

To passing waifs

To challenge Fear?

 If suddenly you leap

Fur blown, tail coiled,

To stare at those outside;

Timid heart beating,

Rapidly,

Like starting deer?

I question....

What makes you so afraid

Of your own kind?

I cherish

This growing love and trust

That calm beside

Such large, gross animals you lie;

So small,

Yet calm,

As they caress you

Lovingly,

Silk chimera,

Gentle –

To such bulk grown blind....

Wrong Side of a Saxophone.

Wrong side of a saxophone –

The bright side –

Reflecting pictures

Of the world,

Surrounding mesh and play

Of colour planes

Incandescent with light....

You rarely see that side.

The side we're shown,

Intricate always,

Myriad pipes, rods, buttons –

Gadgets!

Neat little details

Lose us in the maze

And in that maze

We lose the light –

The side that artists

Love to see....

Delight!

Simple, whole,

Unsullied –

Reflecting life

As life would have us be....

The bright side –

Wrong side of the saxophone!

Vision

From the forest glade,

Gentle,

On the wings of birdsong,

Whispered words....

Enticing....

"Come, join me...."

There was no day or night,

No shade,

No future, and no past,

As now but all eternity....

So with these words

Love beckoned,

Time stood still -

Joy dancing,

Naked shimmering beauty

In Love's light....

Waiting for the light....

Here, in this quiet place,

I hold you.

Though we're apart in time and space

Safe arms enfold you.

There is no room for doubt,

No more my will to fight;

Loving you fills each moment

With such tender light,

Warming my heart and soul

Until our time is right –

Glad now I never told you....

Glad that I never forced Love's pace,

I will me

Always to share this light of grace –

Love will not kill me!

Yours, if you ever need me,

Lover or simply friend;

Keeping all options open

Thus our hearts will mend,

Each act of faith and hope

To you, with joy I send,

That is enough to thrill me....

Tidying Up!

A week moving furniture!

Carpets lifted,

Dust removed,

Chairs moved room to room –

A sofa disembowelled

New one installed,

And then

The MESS....

 Cupboards laid waste!

Discarded blankets

And clothes for Oxfam –

Once comfortable,

Now too loose,

Too tight –

Too old....

Unwanted presents

Laid to rest,

Papers recycled,

Documents shredded

And statements

Burned....

Busy, busy, busy!

The place WAS home,

But only just....

Testament to the madness

They call Spring cleaning –

Blitzing the place....

Yes!

More like THE Blitz!

Seeking a saner pace,

A homely space,

I found the old box –

In the hallway,

By the bathroom door.

Inside,

More papers,

Plastic bottles for recycling

Cardboard folded

Ripe for binman's harvest.....

Scrabbling around,

Rummaging through carrier bags,

The object of my search

Is clear!

Out with the old box!

Upend it!

Contents disgorge

In an interesting heap....

Much better now!

Into the box for me,

I purr myself to sleep....

Love from the ashes....

Here, in this time of healing,

There will be no pain –

No room for doubt –

We show despair the door

As Love we share....

And, in this time of Love,

Will be no loss, but gain

In strength and hope –

Each day, new dawning joy

Will banish care....

As from the ashes of our fears

New songs of Love arise

New promises and faith re-born,

Love, with Her gentle wings,

Will brush away all tears

And lead us to the Light –

Reflected in our eyes –

As smiling now we greet each dawn....

A Wild Rose....

Overwhelming now,

This Love

Surrounding me,

Piercing the veil of sadness....

A small red flower

Lifts its head

Tentatively,

Through clinging green,

Dark,

Rampant,

Clothing an old tree

In the country park....

I bend,

Breathe in its essence,

Fragrance light and sweet

Among the darker woodland smells.

Do you wonder also

At its presence,

Wild,

Untended,

So late in the year?

Autumn's unexpected gift,

A wild rose braves darker days –

For all is well

And ever was...

And will be....

Time stood still....

Time stood still

In the endless days

Of childhood.

Joy it was

To run free!

Remember

The rough and tumble,

Wild and happy,

In the neighbourhood?

Jokes shared,

And endless laughter,

Silly giggling

At nothing

But laughter itself?

How long a wait

Until tomorrow?

Breathing the light,

The air,

The innocence....

Every moment a lifetime!

Every day a new adventure!

Behind bars,

Other children

Are penned,

Like animals,

Indiscriminately,

With criminals and abusers.

Alone in a crowd

Of angry strangers

Where steel bars

Clip their wings....

They cannot fly

They are not strong enough

To fight....

Each moment a lifetime!

Each day an eternity!

Don't tell me

"Youth is wasted on the young"

Rise up and tell them –

Set the children free!

This Day

This day, I will to live

Free from the chains

That bind to errors of the past –

Nor find one grain of fear

In future days unknown and vast –

But exercise my will to give....

This day, I will to love

Complete and whole;

With dreams of waking in a world

Where themes of hope and peace

Reveal Love's flower of Joy unfurled

In Heaven here - not far above....

This day, I will to Be

All that I Am;

To know an inner peace anew

That shows we all are One

Reflecting Love in all we do –

This wisdom now can set us free!

So....

Soft words sung to silent walls

And hung with stars

Flow sweetly in the arms of night....

I see such scars in light of day –

Light so stark, you stand alone,

Where tender dreams seem foolish lies,

Cannot sustain....

I sing the beauty in your soul

And mourn the lack of time-

Your plight –

A trap that holds you fast

Where love and laughter

Wear a veil of pain....

So freely would I give

To win your heart at last!

So lightly brave

The maelstrom tide

To swim and hold you safe,

And thus we live!

So, gladly share the burden

That now weighs you down?

It is not mine to take,

But yours alone to leave.

So -

Sad and silent, stand aside

And watch you drown?

Unless you free your soul to rise

And rising know me as I am,

Love radiant in those eyes?

Believe – only believe –

And love yourself....

You see?

Beloved by God,

Loved by so many,

Cherished – for all time –

By me....

The Unknown, the Unknowable....

The air I breath,

Resonant with your Love,

Will sustain me in this.

This inner peace,

Tranquility itself,

Lends powers to my spirit.

Surrender no more a challenge,

I hitch my soul to a sparrow's wing

And, trusting, fly

Wherever Love will take me....

Losing the way to find the truth....

Losing the path

In gentle hills,

Spirit afire

When Sun streams through

The living canopy of leaves.

Light plays my senses,

Green hued Summer promise

Gold drenched Autumn leaves

And sweet desire....

I am not lost,

Just passing time,

A state of grace –

Confusion's gift....

Remembrance? How I lost my way?

For Life's directions missed,

Love lends reprieve in wonder;

Heart too awed to stray

From such a place....

Sometimes in the night....

Sometimes in the night

Your vision fades and cold dreams

Draw down darker sight....

Feel you close the door....

Am I too near? Too distant?

Could I love you more?

Then Reason assures

We are all One,

And Love will set us free

To see our Sun....

Come to me silent

Love, come to me softly,

Catlike, from the silent darkness -

Redemption shining

In the hour of giving.

From such brooding trees

Your song will come -

Which path you tread
I cannot say…

What sadness fractures living?
This innocence so taken
They also stole from me
In ignorance - for we are One…
Radiant through it all
Still shines such beauty –
To take my breath away
When Understanding sees…

Hidden from cold sight,
Your Love so dared and won -
Though once betrayed,
You seek the Light…
So lay your head, Love,
Soft dreaming upon
This Pillar of Trust I give –
Darkness speaks no more,
Holds no more sorrow
Now Life has begun…

The Only Death Is Fear....

Death is not to cease to Be –

We cannot cease

Though some may try –

Death is suppression

Of the Will to Rise,

Submission to our Fear -

The Ultimate of Lies.

 Death is not the end of Self –

Self does not cease,

But on it flies

To seek expression

By what means it may.

Repressing Love and Joy

Obscures this Living Way.

Death of Fear will conquer All....

Denial of Love

Must cease to be

The chain that binds us

To our hollow lives,

Releasing Love to gain

Our New Reality.....

New World!

Love,

Through a child's eyes

Grown new born awareness

And acceptance of old longings.

Magic,

The red house –

Glowing magnificent

Nestled among the green.

Touch,

Unreal but so imposing!

Rich vista!

Ruby pageant

Shining triumphant!

Who dares such vibrance

In this quiet space

To stir the pallid dullness

Of the village school?

In one step,

The house is grey....

Light

Plays audacious tricks

Compounded by copper beech.

Retrace my steps and gaze again....

Home,

Swift through country lanes –

Pedal to the floor!

Gems –

Emeralds and diamonds –

Love trips the light fantastic

Through a canopy of trees –

Green guard of honour!

What power steers my world?

It takes my breath away –

No turning back....

New world!

Bejewelled with light,

Adorned with Life!

Petit Moineau....

Sometimes

In winter-dark streets

The Impossible

Dreams itself into fruition....

Sweet rain,

Drifting veil,

Softly haloes glowing lamplight.

Smile,

For in this moment

All is known –

All that Is,

And all is won....

One in the Magic Dance

Of light and shadow.

From alley-pitched blackness

Mellows timeless incandescence –

Heart bursts forth in song.

Rain-distant Cathedral

Rings Angelus in rapt mind.

Haunting, fragile,

The little sparrow –

Drab and Promethean –

Coquettish....

Eternal....

Rises from the street;

Soars unbound,

Unbidden,

To new heights!

One Dream

Come now

Within the well of silence;

Time to hold each heart

At peace with Life....

See how the Stars shine on?

The Rain falls sweet?

The Air breathes Joy to taste?

All Life is in me

All is One, none stand alone,

Come now, come Life, make haste....

Come Life

Within the Heart of giving

Learn to sing awhile

In tune with Love....

Pure Love can never die;

It only grows

So, radiant, let it shine

Love has no end, no limit

If we own its Call to Freedom,

Forge no chains on heart and mind....

Come Love

Take up the Call to Oneness;

All shall find new Joy –

At One with Dreams....

There find eternal Light!

See how it shines so brightly?

We shall know no tender separation –

Past illusions fade – dream on,

Dare bolder Dreams, and dreaming grow....

Questions....

Are we so fragmented?

So afraid to come together

In eternal dance of Life?

What past decisions

Led us to Our separation?

What will it take

To make us One

And whole again?

How long the trial?

What do we fear that lies

Upon the straight and narrow path,

That bids us

Take the crooked edge

In fond avoidance?

Know that I love

With all my soul

That part of You in Me –

And Me in You!

If ever joined,

We'll burn the Heavens

With Joy –

As incandescent Suns

Aflame with Love and Light

To own Eternity....

Lifting the Veil

Love's Wings lifted the veil!

So much of pain I let go free

And then such Grace received!

Now, loving, I walk tall and fear no Ill....

My heart is Mine to give it All

When Time is right;

For I Am Love,

So love will seek, shall find,

And lead me dancing to the Light!

I Am that I Am

This is me –

So silent in this hour

Of gentleness –

Too shy to speak of dreams

Or fly rich possibilities,

My hopes,

Flags on a golden helm

As I sail for stars

In faith of future harvest....

This is all –

Fond dreaming in the night...

In love and truth

My pen spins cloth of gold,

Will weave responsibility

For change

With Love and honesty,

Then softly drift

On tides of Trust to sweeter mooring....

November Sun

November sun streams through the trees;

Quicksilver Essence – life, rebirth –

Emerald, gold and jade the leaves –

And silver – eulogy for Mother Earth.

Rubies – holly berries – dance aflame

Within a rich crowned canopy of thorns

And amethyst, dark liquor long since drained.

Sun through sapphire dapples velvet lawns....

Freedom gives us Grace to conquer pain.

Life is for living! Gladly now I see

How impotent the Sun is without rain,

At One with Love, content to simply Be....

As letting go has drawn me close to You

How can I fail to dance through Life anew!

In the Wood....

Sky....

Soft....

Fragrant as roses

In the golden glow of Autumn.

Sun....

Caressing leaves,

Whispers through trees aflame;

My heart afire

With long forgotten dreams....

Light,

Radiant as a smile,

Bursts through

Tentative dawn mist -

My earthbound Soul reborn ....

Happiness....

Catch me if you can!

Brighter than any star,

I fall into your hands

Caressing as I trickle through

These golden sands of Time....

Paler than any

Silver tongued Moonrise

In the lazy Autumn

Hazy, full of richness

In the azure skies.

Hold me if you can….

Wilier than the fox

I'll weave my magic

Wriggle free of chains that bind -

Cold steals from weary hearts -

I'll coax from troubled mind

True promise

Of Love's gentleness –

Lazy, in the moment

Of Time's subtle kiss!

And when you see me rise

To part the mists of pain

Then you shall see Me as I Am,

And understand

The sparkle in my eyes.

In All, with All, Life set me free!

As One, I never looked for ties –

Was ever called to simply Be.

So, catch me if you can –

As I lift you, you nourish me….

A Year Full Circle....

Veiling innocence,

Cold, yet comforting,

Glacial presence;

So strangely gentle,

This soft down blankets my world

Obscuring November's hazy morning sun....

Shine silvery through the transient mists –

As you, I have been numb....

Full circle,

Free cycle,

Another year on the Wheel;

But do I choose to be so racked?

Or loose my grip –

Go spinning wild and free?

Know once I did not dare –

Losing made space to Be.

Reborn,

I win no glittering prize of passion

But a deeper Love

And knowledge locked within....

Recycle?

I will not relive through the years

Old fears and fairy-less tales,

Nor dance with fireflies

Through a Night of pain....

Relinquishing control –

Life's old illusion –

I hitch my soul in trust

To this pale rising star

Still hazy through

The Autumn's frozen kiss.

Retreat –

Surrender to an inner voice

So cradled in Love's healing arms

Awaiting change without or growth within.

Let go....

Accepting,

Come what may....

Become a blazing Sun!

Cat

Stretched out

On cold street furniture

Where sorry hands have laid

In final dream,

I hardly see

Grey on fawn and brindled grey –

So calm you seem....

Beneath

Your welcoming length

One word....

No litter here

Snug, trusting –

Comfort thrusting into

Silken warmth -

Here sleeping loss and fear.

An instant,

I am Cat –

But let it go.

To take your pain,

To seat and ride my own,

What would I gain

Through transference?

Love,

Only Love,

Shone in your eyes –

Yet open, but unseeing.

Still in sweet trust

This Winter day

Stretched now

Before a warming fire,

In dreams you chase and play

Your litter at your breast

Returning to the Light

Within us all

Perhaps, for some,

To rest;

For others,

Show the way....

Seasons in the Fire....

When Spring Sun

Knew no time to breathe -

Love not an option -

Somehow She nurtured growth

And touched my heart,

Brought forth such song!

Then, haunting, turned to leave....

My Summer Sun,

Living in joyous fire

Stayed but awhile,

Then left for fairer climes

Comfort lay in shade

Retreating into self,

Reliving old desire....

When Autumn Sun

Appeared in bleaker days

My dreams took flight.

In openness and trust

I held the Light,

Still standing tall,

My chastened heart ablaze....

Now Winter Sun

Hones gems from leaves grown old,

My inner Sun

Still holds my soul in loving arms,

Cradling tired flame

Until new Light,

New Spring, dispels the cold....

Perfect Day

It's such a perfect day....

Rain showers my windshield,

Mud flies in abandon.

I drive slowly,

Paying attention

To each sly bend in the river

Of glistening tarmac –

I'd like to spend it with you....

Oh! It's such a perfect day....

Bashful children guiltily smile,

Red faced, but eager,

Practice a legend,

Music forgotten,

Yet obediently play

Bright Yuletide songs....

They just keep me hanging on....

And you keep me hanging on

Through the bliss of inner sunshine;

Snatched free time walking

Through rain-scoured streets

Gilt framed with fiery golden charm

Of Autumn hedgerows

And vibrant living conifer green.

Cold wind bids me

Turn my collar

Yet promises the snug warmth

Of my Spartan workroom.

Timid rays creep smiling,

Bashful as clumsy children,

Between drizzling clouds;

Foretaste of a bold parade

Through golden guard of honour

On winding, tree-lined lanes.

Fresh air! Fresh joy! Fresh puddles

To skim in silent laughter

On this,

My journey into blithe instruction....

You just keep me hanging on

In Faith, in Love, in Gratitude –

Such a Perfect Day!

Fog Shrouds the River at Boston.

Soft,

Blow smoke rings

Into my silver downtime –

Framing hazy Sun

In mist, upon mist,

Through freezing air....

Bold,

Yet gentle,

Blue tinged ribbon of silk

Laps ancient moorings

In flow, upon flow,

Past silver railings there....

White,

Hang snowflake silhouette

On steely tide –

Lone spider's web,

A star adorned in morning dew,

Too pure and beautiful to hide....

Sometimes....

Sometimes

I wonder where you are....

Not in the City;

Too fine in the hustle

Of human plight....

Then I catch

The sound of laughter,

Flash of light -

The pulse of neon -

Bright on the skyline....

Not in these country lanes

I must pursue;

Stop!

Wind down the window;

Then I taste the scent of rain

And hear the mystic music of birds

And silence....

Not here,

Where I smell sweet fragrance

And, dreaming, rest my head

Where once you lay....

Not in my silent room;

Yet silence sets the scene

To play awhile and you awake

My inner smile and make my day....

I'm lost and found in finding you

Somehow I know

When speaks my solitude -

Why wonder where you are?

I feel you all around

You're with me everywhere I go....

I wait in trust

I wait in trust for times

That will not pass me by

As stranger,

Through mist of long confusion

Tinged with brandy tears.

 Unwise to dwell on wasted years....

Oblivious to danger,

Throw my heart unfathomed

Into channelled rhymes –

And hope to still my fears,

Each minute an eternity....

Each second full as it can be!

In life

Where springs the hope?

This love I feel

With all my soul?

From simple things?

In company with those

Who cannot understand?

For now alone -

Long furrow ploughed in pain

From which I seek to nurture peace

In trust and solitude so vast;

These words that leave my hand

For all to see

Ring true, sing strong and proud

In heartfelt gratitude at last

That I…. am me…

Today

Sky crying freely,

Unfettered

Like my child within.

Rain scours farm cheeks

And worry lines

Of country lanes….

Resting now,

Car cradled in the Wolds,

Listening to silence….

Wind evokes wild geese

Through whipping aerial....

Lured by siren song,

I dream secure

In my haven....

Sky tears -

Salt sea spray

Lashing rolling deck -

Wash Night away;

Leaving me blessed,

Warm,

Safe in loving arms

Of Inner Self....

Today I know,

I feel,

I Am....

New Year's Eve.

Feel sharp clarity,

This last December sun

Bites through my fingers

Where melting snows run....

Time alone may hide –

With still, white veil on skyline –

Laughing yesterdays thrown warm

Into welcoming arms of snow....

City-self clothed in white,

Lay low in tender innocence

Fine and pure as a virgin bride....

Now, bold with resolution,

Dare I fly through life

Into the New and brave Unknown!

Love's wings will lift,

Release from pain,

And life returns to frozen hands

Relaying from the heart of love

New dreams, from old, now born again!

Tonight I love

Tonight I love

With gentleness of spirit

And let my soul take wing

In Oneness now and joy of it....

I would not say

The way you fill each hour; and yet

The peace you bring with radiant smile

Is something sacred

I cannot forget....

So, let me dance

This highway of my being

Where, somehow awed, I sing

In honest faith for clearer seeing.

Tonight I pray

Allow my dreams are whole -

Within one perfect moment's span,

To be content

In heart, in mind and soul....

Stardust born

Love, in this stillness

Might I dream

You know me as I Am?

As born of golden silence

Words flow soft as clouds,

Caress the skies....

Now in the Moment,

Freedom flies the soul's release

And bursts all mortal bars.

Love, as I Am -

In dream of Oneness -

Stardust born in peace

Returns to touch the stars....

Divine Beauty

Listen!

Gently birdsong

Penetrates the veil of human mind.

Such music never dies!

So, silent drifting,

Simply Be the Song

And close your eyes....

Beauty found me sleeping....

Dreaming,

I found Love and rainbows

Chased my soul to noble height;

All in the Moment

Heard Love call

And saw the Light!

Beauty

Within us all,

This Essence of the Now,

Begin to find

One vision call us home....

Love is not lost when All is One,

We only win as in Life's scheme

We know, we see,

We dare to Be the Beauty –

Fearless in our destiny

To Feel the Dream –

The mystery, Divine, of Love within....

Surreal Duality.

These,

My Lincolnshire Mountains –

Morning solid clarity –

Stillness reassuring....

Depth of purple heather, gorse aflame,

Tree line grey – fine reality....

Snowline sun-flashed brilliance

Bursts slipstreamed skies!

Stay with me always, my Electric Sun,

Radiance dazzling my eyes

Can do no harm;

I dare to see, you show me how....

Clouds form dreamscape –

Inner light unfurled –

Surreal duality....

Here within my world –

So comforted –

Souls touching in the Now

Become as One....

Now Love's echoing stillness

Now Love's echoing stillness

Drifts soft through Being....

Here, as I am

Sheltered, eternal shade,

I trust the waves

On which I rock....

There is no end;

But freeing

All I am through you

To fear no shock....

So in my stillness -

Come to me as friend -

I sail on fearless

Through remaining days.

Future unknown,

Past nurtured,

Present I own

In love alone

To Be amazed....

As Future Time....

As Future Time must pass and fade

Here in the moment,

Past forgot,

Forgive all errors made....

Deep in the heart of meaning –

Storm scoured Sea unchanged,

Rain captive now release to fill again,

To swift concede in flux

Receding tide of pain –

All live for change

In light and shade!

Love cannot cease to Be;

Will never hide forgiving Grace

Where fear of silence bowed to Faith

To rise and boldly face the Now –

Yet face it Free –

So future days and past,

But never Love,

Would pass and fade....

The Unicorn

Soft nestling safe among trees,

And always in my thoughts with you,

Snowy foretaste hanging in the breeze

As Sun breaks through grey skies anew.

Light's pattern leaves me breathless, dumb,

At country splashed with emerald green

A distant, and hypnotic hum

Lures thoughts of dragons to the scene

And in this moment silence torn

A horse emerges from the glade

For one split second, Unicorn,

And then as quickly vision fades....

But feeling you with me in subtle mind

More wonderful than Unicorns, I find....

Blazing....

Ten thousand lifetimes,

Searching,

Now I win eternity....

My golden Sun burns proudly –

In her truth stands tall....

So, stars blazing brightly

All are mine to see,

To touch....

To feel one drop of hope,

One dream, one seed of faith,

Outshine them all!

And in this Love

You light my way

To clear

The mist of time in trust;

So dare I chide at pain

And say,

I will not fear

Though bend I must....

From Darkness Reborn....

Breathless on the bridge....

Wind whips scour incoming tide;

Fine rain scatter on the river –

Sand blasted aimless in its flow.

Reverse flow,

Against the grain

As was my life....

Cold cuts a fresh remembrance

Of pale death –

Crucifixion of spirit....

Yet now, at last, I rise,

Greet Dawn with open smile,

Trusting soul reborn in pure surrender,

Asking nothing more than this;

Awake, to search your Dreamtime

For a new reality –

On sleeping eyes

Plant love's enduring kiss....

Come to me....

Come to me.... Come to me.... Come to me.... Come to me....

Come to me.... Come to me.... Come to me.... Come to me....

Come to me (Come to me....)

With the sound of rainbows in your hair

With a taste of summer rain

On my heart weave velvet chains

Only Heaven can compare.

Come to me (Come to me....)

In my arms find warmth and dignity

Take me to a foreign shore

So my Sun will shine once more

In the Oneness our souls share.....

And when you lay your head again

Upon my pillow

Whisper softly

That you'll take away the pain,

That this life is not in vain,

Bending willow,

Whisper to me.....

Come to me.... (Come to me....)

Speak of life and not finality

Say you'll never go away,

Play the games the lovers play,

Won't you bend to my reality.....

Come to me.... Come to me.... Come to me.... Come to me....

Come to me.... Come to me.... Come to me.... Come to me....

And when you lay your head again

Upon my pillow

Whisper softly

That you'll take away the pain,

That this life is not in vain,

Bending willow,

Whisper to me.....

Come to me,

Lay your burdens on my satin dreams

And you'll never want for more,

Bending willows know the score

Riding storms with whispered themes....

Under the Apple Tree....

Under the apple tree was never easy –

Nor was I ever young....

In those far off days of Summer,

I swear, the hours were long

And dark dreams longer.

I shut my heart,

Sought comfort in the gift of song,

So, numb, I played an alien part

Lived in perpetual haze

Till I grew stronger....

Then, under those same boughs

I set me free and danced awhile –

Oh! I was beautiful in you

When apples blossomed!

Then dared to smile

And dreaming light,

I caught a glimpse of me –

Young now, and laughing easy, beautiful,

Content in Being, blissful Being True....

Midnight, Lincoln, 23rd March 2006

How can I love you more

Each minute of each passing day?

How melt again

With every image,

Every word I hear you say?

Your words, my spirit, mingle

Touching heart and soul,

Sing Hope and Joy,

And exorcise what's past.

No loss -

And no more need to fight.

Our only Truth?

As One,

This Heaven we gain

When sweet at last we realise

From darkness

Always shines Love's light,

Dispelling all illusions -

Lies of grief and pain....

Thirty years on....

(For Jewels)

And when I say I love you

Will they chase this dream?

Pour doubt on innocence

To drive a sleeping heart

Back into frozen wastes of Time?

I bend to kiss your sleepy eyes

Within my Dream and know

No way, nowhere, no need to hide

The passion or the beauty

Of each moment spent with you....

Within this silent twilight

Of Time's separation

There can be no End

But only bold awakening –

Beginnings have their own finality!

Thus, when I say I love you

They will learn to love an inner self

In all its infinite joy

Reborn from oh, such calm reality!

Love's Renewal.

Take in this Moment All I Am

However vague or pale it seems;

Know Who I Am renewed in You –

Creating substance of my Dreams....

Think in this Moment by my side

As All I Am I freely give

Once shared, Love cannot be lost -

It is sole reason that We live!

In leaving this our Past behind

To face our Future, one sweet kiss

Can unify our Heart and Mind

Divine in our eternal bliss….

So take to the Dance – eternal now – Life has begun

And in this Dance – the Dance of Love – know We Are One!

Birthday….

The not so tender touch

Of half a lifetime

In the dark

I never mourn nor miss.

Things vainly hoped but lost

Led to much greater bliss.

Full years I carry light -

Life never burdens -

This I know!

Such wisdom gained, so long

Confirmed by Love's sweet kiss,

I celebrate in song.

And knowing who I am

At last Life's meaning

Comes to state

In confidence, so bold,

That Love can do no wrong

And sometime must be told

To those I know and love

Who cannot fathom

Heart unknown

Cold spanning fifty years -

That now must break the mould,

Refuse to own salt tears....

In fifty years I learn

Love does not follow

Others' words

Disdaining to be sung

But longs to shed all fears –

And in that shedding

Grow forever young....

For All....

And through Cherry Blossom snowstorms

I will hold the hand

That guides me through

These troubled times....

In mind,

I call your name

And see you smile!

Find words

That seemed in hiding,

So long

In the darkness

Of my lifelong Winter....

Where were you?

I would call

Within my inner self

Feeling rehearsal

Cold for warmer times,

My Jewels, we now await!

And when we meet

Perhaps for those

Who could not love,

And Love

For those

Who could not live,

Then shall we know

These gifts that made us One,

For All as One -

Is One for Love,

We plan

Forever....

In the Forest.

Spellbound....

In the soft beyond of now

Love bids me wake!

I sing my truth

And take sweet breath of you;

Heart beating reckless

In its timid knowing,

Nervous like a deer.

Yet oh so bold this dream

Under your forest roof -

Tall trees

Beside a waterfall!

Love bids me kiss

Sweet distant lips -

Nor miss the touch

For touch so near

As of the soul

Can never closer be....

Two hearts as One,

Within this frame

See how

All Time and Space

Is won....

Spellbound....

Within the soft beyond

Of Now,

My Love –

Your own....

Rachmaninov

Breeze –

Green whispered memory

Of long distant April....

Life spilling Spring Tide

Over Emerald Hills

Wherein I lose myself

And washing over me!

Will my heart burst

Riding waves of Love,

As once so long ago

Drowning within surge

And wild rush of bliss?

Forgetting Time and Task

In Tears of Joy

You're with me yet so far.

Though rich,

All Dreams must wait,

Intense as colour in the Hills.

Apart we are, yet so together!

Kiss to Wake....

(For my darling Woolly Bear)

Oh! Wake up do!

Ten o'clock looms,

I dreamed such dreams

And now I kiss

Tired eyes to dream

Of Saturdays to come!

Such games we'll play,

Such sweet dancing,

Pouncing bold to laugh

Upon some too big ball of string.

My Love, oh, wake up do!

Somewhere you wait -

You rule my days,

My Goddess,

Miss no detail of each moment

In such fond embrace!

Arms forged in Heaven,

Falling into Trust,

And chasing laces into Love....

The Faerie Ring

If I could bring you roses' touch

Of finest damask silk and vibrant hue

Such scent of love to greet you

As the Dawn Rise in my sky....

If I could catch each moment's care

And bind it with such happiness as Love so true

Infect all worlds with laughter innocent

'Til every subtle grief should fade and die....

These would I do for Love!

But 'til that day?

From darkness shine such diamonds

Bold these sapphires royal surprise

To dance a faerie reel across our night as Stars

Remind me of the Love that's in your eyes!

Simply Beautiful

Simply beautiful

The way you are;

Your Summer sunlight,

Silver moonshine,

Chased dark night away

Made my heart leap in joy

To know you're mine!

Simply beautiful

The way I am

As my Love sings

Within your presence,

Knowing darker things

Must fade to slumber

In Love's innocence....

Simply beautiful!

In Truth we stand as One

All once Unknown and Deep

Must shine as Beacon

To the Power of Trust!

Another Monday....

November calls again –

This time in Trust –

This bold electric Sun my own!

Where once such manic dreams

Lay unfulfilled and desolate

My smile betrays a subtle warmth -

Love's sweeter glow -

As Mission City slumbers

Peaceful under snow....

November calls again –

As call it must –

Stiffly as a hedgehog see me stir,

Escape this prickly ball

Wherein I lay so long.

Relaxing, stretch, lie easier now.

Defenceless? BOLD!

For Love needs build no barriers

When Truth be told!

And, as I stretch limbs stiff

From lack of warmth

Bright Sun steals hibernation

From dull Winter's eyes....

Soft realise in smile

The role that Winter plays;

Heart open once again,

Renewed in fond embrace

Of joyful Summer Days....

Ironic....

Ironic this reflection

Of a "me" I do not know!

So do I view myself as others see?

Or did another sow the doubts

And fears you heaped on me?

I never owned the sad reflection

That you thoughtless cast aside!

Ironic what I did to please

Should warp my image so!

Even in Truth, you said I lied....

Ironic this reflection, friend,

You said I never knew you –

And all the time I loved you

Seems that I was looking through you!

And even though I wept

Because we'd never meet again

Ironic my reflection

Should despise me for the pain....

Strange

How Fog shields

Before She lifts....

Soft, cushioning,

She blankets this,

Our world,

And softens hard reality

With insulating kiss....

So pierce the veil?

Confront your truth head on

And laugh insane

At hidden chaos?

See beyond Her glory,

Kind confusion steering lives apart,

Land laid naked –

Led from grief in joy!

Enshrine Fog's wild illusion -

Cold, yet comforting!

Hearts once healed

Have no more need of answer -

Know no purpose more than Love –

And nor does She....

Through clearing, cleansing Fog we see!

Not Fog that madness kissed,

Yet we are One -

And dancing Innocent -

Once woken by the silence

Of December's golden Sun!

Fable

She moved like a butterfly....

Rainbow in flight

Love was her truth

Her beauty was whole.

She moved like a butterfly....

Drawn to the light

A free dancing moth

Her lone sister soul.

Together they danced

In amazing reflection.

Moth blazed forth colours

Of new-born perfection -

And butterfly feared

Seeing Love set so free

She danced like a butterfly....

Stung like a bee!

New Year Comes

New Year comes,

And with it sound of sirens....

Fireworks blast my ears

To rude awakening....

This special time

I hold you yet so dear

As each and every day

A New Day starts,

Another year begins....

New Year comes,

And now I sit and ponder

Fireworks prompt

A heart to smiling recognition....

This special year

I gave myself to Love

Such Love as each and every

New Year holds

And touches warm....

Another Year,

Another Space and Time,

A chance for learning....

Yet each day, each glimpse

Of futures present,

Glories past and sorrows fled,

Was present from the First

No resolutions,

Only Love – that's All....

One

Sometimes in moments

When we touch the stars

We know all in an instant

That was meant to Be,

Releasing to an Ocean of Eternity

Our frail need to know....

Sometimes in an instant

Fly the soul into the Infinite,

Touch the Face of One-ness –

Call it God –

Then like a skimming stone,

Or speeding bullet,

Drop back to the world below....

Sometimes the drop

Into our bold humanity

Can seem so brave

A leap from intuition in the dark,

And yet as One we rise again

To surface brave and bold,

And reap the Love

We learn to sow....

Forgiveness

This year warm;

As snowdrops pierce the veil

And early blossoms pale

Take form in virginal hedgerows,

Soft with improbability,

Sun rays warm my heart

In bright forgiveness

Of all past insanity....

Where would I be but for your Love?

Intended?

Lying easy

In Spring's openness?

Untended?

Drifting wild upon the Path

The Universe bids bless!

I'm done!

I'm free!

With eyes new open,

Only now I see!

All Hallows

I miss you

In the silence

Of the bright October sun.

I miss you in the peace

That reason

Lent me just to Be

I miss your sparkling laughter

And the shyness of your smile,

But most of all

I miss your call

To find a better part of me.

Late sunlight,

Brightly streaming,

Lends bright leaves a faery glow

The stillness of All Hallows

Rising in the sacred grove

So close we are today

And yet too soon must come

The time to part…

But know that now I'm found

I never will be far away….

Amazing Classic Cars….

From village unto village,

Café, shop, and school

Amazing classic cars

Patrol the Wolds.

Right eye scans the road ahead

And left eye scans the guage

The radiator sneaks a hiss - but holds!!!!

Now slow to join the convoy

As the chips are down,

We stall;

We switch her off

To spare the leaks

And summon bliss!

Floating over fields –

My spirit soars with ease

Silver sheen on velvet nap

Of blue green barley.

And can I bend

Caressing silken fur

Soft rippling in the breeze?

As land lies purring,

Over undulating hills,

Grown sleek...

My Golden Sun

Springs into Life,

Burns warm,

Brings Love's embrace

To seize Land's nape

And brighten

Pin prick vestiges

Of blossom in the rape!

Journey's end

And foxglove ushers

Greet the cars,

Saluting florid roses

Boast and blaze...

Above a haze of white

A green familiar ghost

Now delicately shades

Sweet alpine flowers,

An MG parked quiescent

Guards through cherished hours

Earth's virginal reflection

Of the stars...

A whisper of the Romantic....

(For Jewels)

Tonight

Shall I chase flickering logs

From frost to remembrance?

Or watch a guttering candle

Dance from eye to eye

Soft comforting all waking dreams

To journey forth

Or, wistful, spry?

No well of loneliness

But of our making....

As much my body misses

Sweet caresses

Once it only dared to dream,

My heart aflame, my soul lies tranquil

In Love's arms of sweet remembrance!

Even now we're One

Inseparable by Oceans in our bliss

A whisper of the Romantic

In the Eye of God....

Alone in the Fens

I love this land…

This field…

This regal carpet…

Tree thrones set in lavender

Greet King Magpie and Queen Rook.

Along the road I look

And yield to fading dreams…

So near and yet so far

The schemes of ill-starred Love!

Great gifts you gave -

I wrote possessed,

Yet grew

Through my insanity…

Now all is fled

Except for freedom,

Calm remembrance

Bled like poppies -

Warm and red

In virgin hedgerows,

Speckled Hemlock white,

Jostled by tall grasses...

Names escape me as you did...

Yet learning freedom's worth,

Knee deep in lavender,

I won my wings at last

To soar o'er purple fields

One warm July

And fly to Love...

Earth Angel

My angel stood tall,

His platinum mane shone bright

As halo to highlight perfect Greek physique.

Half-naked he stood in crystal clear water

Spring Sun dappling the golden torso

Beads of water ran from sculptured muscle.

His hands pulled –

Struggling with a great net –

Such power in the movement,

Such earnest trembling....

Distracted for a moment I wondered

Was he Andrew, or was he John?

Or even Simon Peter?

It mattered not at all!

He was a Fisher of Men,

Ordained so many centuries past!

Strong young arms trembled with exertion,

Strong young hands flailed and shook.

Purposeful, uncoordinated, he waded

Determined eyes cast towards his companions.

He reached the edge of the pool,

Sat there, looked up, conversing with

His companions, the lifeguards....

He was Raphael!

So beautiful in his new found humanity!

Then someone rolled away the chair....

You know it's true what they say—

Angels are always perfect!

No Greater Gift

No greater gift than friendship

Could you give,

Nor greater would I choose;

Past ills forgotten,

Foolishness forgiven,

Nothing else to gain.

The Me you once rejected –

Myth of accidental making –

I would lose

It caused us too much pain!

You, angry, said

"I never knew you"

(Glimpses caught, I loved) –

That hurt,

But greater still,

More than rejection,

Friend, You never knew me...

But through misunderstanding

I walked within your shoes

I sought within your silence

And the silence

Looked right through me....

So now, my friend,

I understand the "Me" you saw,

The "I" she was,

And simply count God's blessings

That neither one was true...

At last I smile in gratitude,

Love helped me find

The soul I'd lost –

I ask all four,

Our friendship we renew.

And When I Leave....

And when I leave this place what will I take?

What leave behind?

Does ownership persist beyond

Detritus of unruly mind?

Eddies of anger furrowed and stormed

Once fertile clay....

Stings of rejection, bitter yet,

And, fond remembered,

Lovers' laughter heals the rift....

So cling now

To this blissful dance of gratitude

Love bid me forth to lead!

Find happiness in simple truth,

Where sustenance of friendship

Lifts the veil of Winter.

Breezes freshen as they chill

Awakening fields of snowdrops

To the early February shift.

Our every morning Sun must set

As evening waits a new rebirth

In salmon streaks, and violet,

Skies richly golden, half moon hazy lies,

The promise of New Dawn on Earth.

All anguish past?

Forget!

Eternal bliss to find

In quiet Buddhahood

And yet more silent, subtle Mind.

Tupholme Abbey

Sun held fire

And moon kissed light of day.

I kissed you

As we lay enshrined

In faery ring…

We broached a metal gate,

I heard a two tone flute –

Deep solo of the wind?

The city long abandoned,

Sound now mute,

Our country opened free

To birdsong.

Odd gathering here,

So busy this, our shrine,

We circled ruins

Biding time until alone -

And then we lay all smiles

To feel the Love in silver circles

Dance for miles!!!

Too soon the call to leave…

Thanksgiving offering left

Within a hollow tree,

The spirits of this holy place

Now set the reeds to silvery dance

And wind to chase in faery glow

To thank us in our turn!

When Sun holds fire,

Moon kissing light of day

As faery kiss on grove

I worship you!

Our Love enshrines a silence

Sacred as this space…

Beyond the rainbow do you sense the midnight black?

Beyond the rainbow do you sense the midnight black?

Here diamonds streak across a velvet sky…

There is

No greater than

No smaller than

No wiser than

No simpler than

And no more beautiful....

We know identity has taught us

We are better than

Some richer than

Some poorer than

Some brighter than

Some lighter than

And we can choose which seeds to sow....

But no! Our separation bids rebirth!

Each day rehearsal for a longer night

Each night a chance to free ourselves and fly

Where some are free

And some are not

And some are head

And some are heart

And all are of the earth....

And so apart,

We fill the vessel with our subtle mind –

The Heart of One –

We learn the way of Love,

We need not shout!

There is no best

No beast, no fall....

What is achieved belongs to All -

And there is no way out!

The Stupa fills with midnight black

A soul embraced by All who would be One

To glimpse Divinity in everything

And loving all as self

In time become Divinity

Beyond the rainbow

As the diamond stars

Chase subtle velvet black....

Complete in my fractured heart

Complete in my fractured heart

I let you go -

Essence of One -

Love that like two blazing Suns

Would soar into eternity....

Such Faith and such Surrender!

Each waking hour was You –

Then Truth, embarrassed, intervened.

Complete in my fractured heart

I let it die

A blaze too strong for hearts to hold;

With Passion, Ego died,

And separation....

Complete in my fractured heart

I let it pass

Into the night of wild dreams and past failures

Mourning darkly for a little while

But gentler words of Love

Had vanquished Death!

So,

Good as you, my fractured heart,

An Innocent reborn,

Made whole by tenderness and Youth regained

Know there is no such dream as failure!

This Love will save all worlds of my own making!

February....

Today....

I am not an archangel foretelling

The birth of Kings of Heaven,

Or Queens of Earth,

I am the wintry white bridal gown

Of hoar on lacy hedgerow.

I am not come to praise

But discipline

Errant snowdrops for indecent haste.

I am foreteller of the Prime Time;

I am the Rime Time.

The Dreamtime where cocooned

In icy angel wings

Subtle warmth diffuses

Rose quartz silence.

I am the way of magic dreams

Where streams of grey

Lie flower bound....

Bordered by asters and orchids of frost,

Where ferns of light's renewal

Recycle dead brown stems

And drier leaves to vibrancy....

Bold headlights beam enchanted dance

Through midnight black

Where paths swim vague

In the dark, in the night,

In the dark, in the out

Of the Hour of Forgetfulness....

I herald no new birth as yet,

But cherish darkly pregnant thoughts

Until life through me runs its course

A force too green to hold

And bursts in Spring's bold sunlight!

A Love too big for hearts to hold....

Flashes of rainbows in the dew on the grass –

Life's ended before it's begun,

But Love hurts only until the grieving is past

For the Soul knows that now we are One.

You'll never leave me – I feel you here in my heart!

Your voice soft and sweet sounds anew

So I must let go of the pain that I feel

I know things are better for you.

A Love too big for hearts to hold

Has taken you away

When your heart failed, then my heart broke,

But our Love forever will stay!

Outside the sun shines, inside the teardrops fall

And I wish I could hold you again.

You know I love you with all my heart and soul

Forever One, and for you no more pain.

And when the rain stops in this heart of mine

I will cherish each memory anew.

The smiles and laughter and the Love that you are

Will help me to hold on to you.

A love too big for hearts to hold

Has taken you away

Though my heart broke when your heart failed

Eternal our Love will remain.

Kestrel.....

Diving headlong into unknown green

Pursues a break in the stillness;

Brakes, banks, grasps on sight and soars again –

Beauty impaled on eager talons

And greeting Death in joyous flight....

So meeting Love,

Headstrong I plunge empowered

Into seas of red

Heedless of the stings,

Petals aflame,

Transforming poppies

Into fragile welts of honour,

Berry stains on pale and tender skin.

Meeting my Divinity in love,

I rise -

Complete and unafraid -

And in the Now beyond Eternity

Where Love and Death unravel

I see that there is only Life!